Guess the Shape

By Amanda Gebhardt

2

Cole and his class play a fun game. It is Guess the Shape.

Cole and his class must
tell shape names.

 "Which shape is this?"
Miss Tran asks.

Cole thinks.
Cole will add up its sides.

 This shape has three sides. "It is a triangle," Cole tells Miss Tran.

"Yes! This is the next shape. Which shape is it?" Miss Tran asks. "Check its sides."

8 It has four sides.

The sides are the same length.

"This shape is a square,"
Pam tells Miss Tran.

"Yes! What is this last shape?"
Miss Tran asks.

 It does not have sides.

"It is a circle!"
The class tells her.

Word List

math words

add	shape
circle	sides
four	square
Guess	three
length	triangle

sight words

a	play
are	square
circle	the
does	three
four	triangle
Guess	What
have	

silent e

Cole	shape	names	sides
game	Shape	same	

Try It!

Find shapes in your class or at home.
Name the shapes.

14

Cole and his class play a fun game.

It is Guess the Shape.

Cole and his class must tell shape names.

"Which shape is this?" Miss Tran asks.

Cole thinks. Cole will add up its sides.

This shape has three sides.

"It is a triangle," Cole tells Miss Tran.

"Yes! This is the next shape. Which shape
    is it?" Miss Tran asks. "Check its sides."

It has four sides.

The sides are the same length.

"This shape is a square," Pam tells Miss Tran.

"Yes! What is this last shape?" Miss Tran asks.

It does not have sides.

"It is a circle!" The class tells her.

Published in the United States of America by Cherry Lake Publishing Group
Ann Arbor, Michigan
www.cherrylakepublishing.com

Cherry Blossom Press is an imprint of Cherry Lake Publishing Group.

Library of Congress Cataloging-in-Publication Data has been filed and is available at catalog.loc.gov.

Cherry Lake Publishing Group would like to acknowledge the work of the Partnership for 21st Century Learning, a Network of Battelle for Kids. Please visit http://www.battelleforkids.org/networks/p21 for more information.

Printed in the United States of America
Corporate Graphics

Amanda Gebhardt is a curriculum writer and editor and a life-long learner. She lives in Ann Arbor, Michigan, with her husband, two kids, and one playful pup named Cookie.